W9-AGD-023

In the Wild
Activity Fun Stickers

Written by Brenda Apsley
Designed and illustrated by Julie Clough

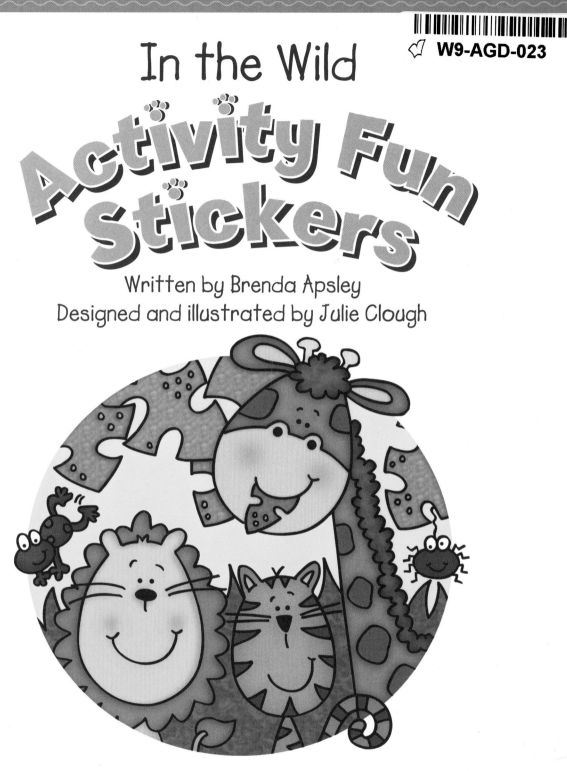

Kane Miller
A DIVISION OF EDC PUBLISHING

BOOKS IN ACTION

First American Edition 2011
Kane Miller, A Division of EDC Publishing
PO Box 470663, Tulsa, OK 74147-0663
First published by Egmont UK Ltd in Great Britain in 2005
Copyright © Egmont UK Limited 2010
All rights reserved
Printed in China
1 2 3 4 5 6 7 8 9 10 • 978-1-61067-016-6
www.kanemiller.com • www.edcpub.com

It's morning, and the animals are having a drink at the watering hole. Draw a big, yellow sun in the sky, and color in the picture. Add some stickers if you like.

How many eggs has the turtle laid? Color in each egg outline you find and write the number in the box.

There are ☐ eggs.

Starting at number 1, connect the dots to complete this big animal, then color in your picture.

Color in the big picture of the toucan, using the small one as a guide.

Read or listen to this hide-and-seek picture story. Finish coloring in the pictures, and tell the story in your own words.

1. "Now, where's that big gorilla hiding?"

2. "Is he in the bush?"

3. "Is he behind the rock?"

4. "Where are you, Gorilla?"

All penguins look alike – or do they? Can you point to the odd one out?

The big bear is fishing for his dinner. Which piece will complete the jigsaw puzzle picture?

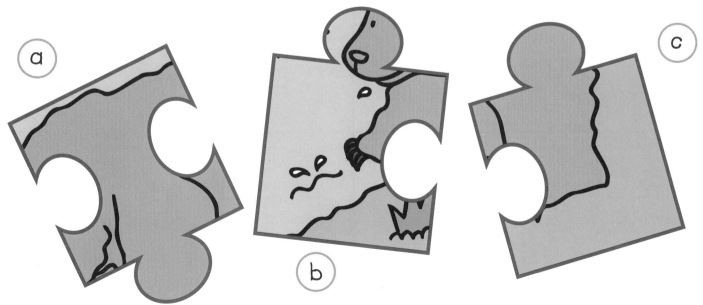

Draw and color in the missing half of each hippo.

Draw lines to match the snakes that are the same.

Eeek! There's a big, hairy spider hanging from the tree! Draw 8 long, hairy legs to complete him – if you dare!

Which one of these animals lives in the desert? Color him in.

camel

cat

beaver

penguin

Answer: camel

Beavers use tree branches to build houses called lodges. They float on the water. Show the beaver the way to the lodge.

Connect the sets of dots to complete the tiger's stripes, and color in his picture using the code.

The pictures on these pages look the same, but 5 things are different in picture 2. Can you spot the differences?

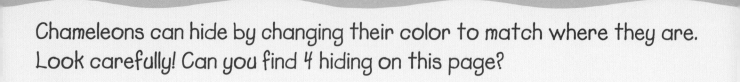

Chameleons can hide by changing their color to match where they are.
Look carefully! Can you find 4 hiding on this page?

Can you guess what this tall animal is? Draw it in one line, without lifting your pencil from the page. Start at the dot and follow the lines.

It is a g_____ .

Use blue to color all the shapes with a blue snowflake in them to see who lives on the ice. Do you know his name?

Copy the picture of the lion square by square, then color it in.
Think of a name for him and write it on the line, then add your name.

_____ the Lion,   by _____

Some animals are very shy, like this antelope who likes to hide in the long grass. Draw and color in lots more leaves and clumps of grass and add stickers if you like.

Can you draw a line to match the dolphin to his shadow?

Listen to or read about how butterflies grow, then tell the story in your own words. Now, finish coloring in the pictures.

1. A caterpillar grows inside an egg.

2. The egg breaks open and the little caterpillar eats and eats.

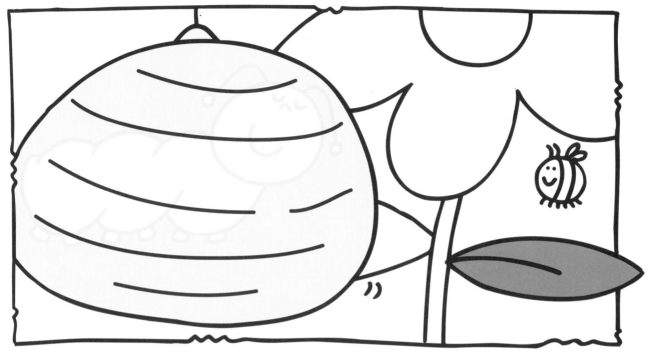

3. The fat caterpillar makes a cocoon and goes to sleep inside.

4. After a while the cocoon splits ... out comes a butterfly!

Count the yellow, purple and red hummingbirds and write the numbers in the flowers.

Can you find the way out of the big spider's web without crossing any lines?

Use black to fill in the parts of the picture with a dot to complete the panda. Draw lots more sticks of bamboo for her to eat.

Draw lines to match the mothers to their babies.

This is a blue whale, the largest animal of all.

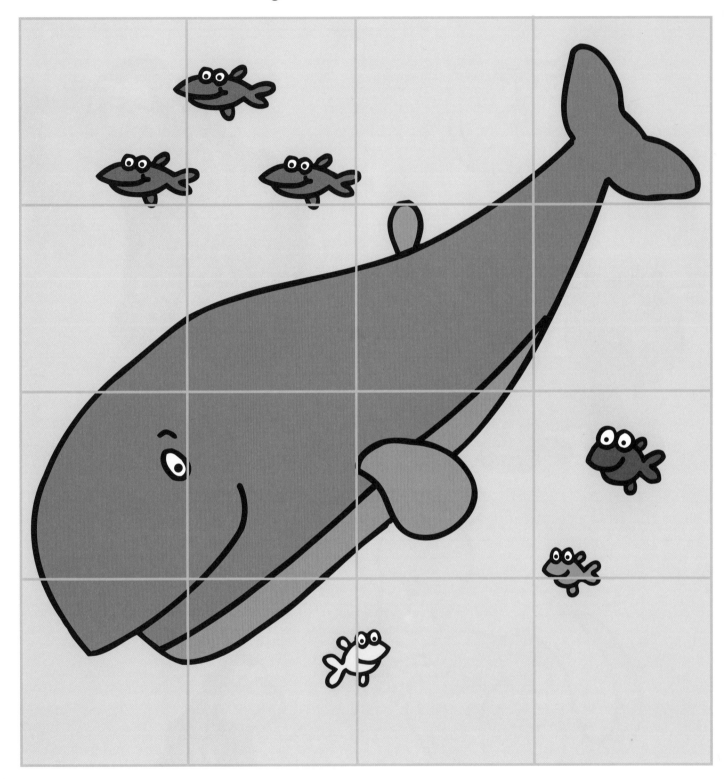

Copy the picture, then give him a name. Write your name on the line, too!

_____ the Blue Whale, by _____

Talk or read about the animals, then draw lines from the words to their pictures.

I can make
a bad smell.

I am a scorpion.

I can sting.

I am a snake.

I can rattle
my tail.

I am a skunk.

Starting at number 1, connect the dots to finish this picture of a big animal with lots of teeth! Do you know its name?

It is a c_____.

Play the animal noises game. Point to an animal and say its name. Now, can you copy the noise it makes?

Lion

Frog

Snake

croak!

roar!

ssss!

Bear

Bird

Crocodile

growl!

snap!

tweet!

"Smile, please!" Color in the photo that matches the picture of the zebra.

Show the seal the way to get to the little island.

Tree frogs have sticky toes so they can climb trees! Can you color in the 6 frogs on the big tree? They are green, with red eyes.

It's very hot in Africa, where lions live. Draw a yellow sun in the sky and a big tree with lots of green leaves to make a shady place for the lion family to rest.

Read or listen to this story about a big lion and a tiny mouse.
Now tell the story in your own words. Remember to make lots of grrrr!
and eeek! noises.

1. One day, a lion met a mouse. "Grrrr!" said the lion.

2. "Eeek!" said the mouse. "Please don't hurt me, and one day I will help you."

3. One day the lion got caught in a net. "Grrrr!" he said. "Help!"

4. "Eeek!" said the mouse, munching through the net.
   "You were kind to me, so I will help you."

Color in this picture of the bright pink flamingos.

Bony antlers grow on the heads of deer like this one. Starting at number 1 each time, connect the 2 sets of dots to give him a big set of antlers.

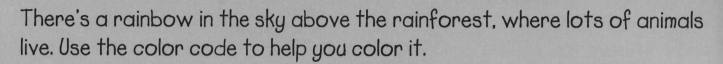

There's a rainbow in the sky above the rainforest, where lots of animals live. Use the color code to help you color it.

Which little monkey is different? Can you find the odd one out?

What a lot of pretty butterflies! Can you find 2 that are exactly the same?

Draw lots of spots on the little leopard cubs. Can you think of names for them all?

It's nighttime in the jungle, and the animals are all asleep – or are they? How many hidden pairs of eyes can you see? Color in the picture. Add some stickers if you like.